FREE

bitly

Unlock Your Free Bonus Book!

As a heartfelt **thank you** for choosing our book, we're delighted to offer you a **FREE book.**

CONTENTS

INTRODUCTION

Max and Lily had been best friends since kindergarten. Now, at 13 years old, they still shared the same love for technology, adventure, and unraveling mysteries. Max was the tech guru of the pair, always seen with his neatly styled hair, a cool headband, and a pair of sleek glasses. He could take apart and reassemble any gadget in record time, and his room was a testament to his passion, filled with electronic parts, tools, and half-finished projects. He loved coding, building robots, and playing the latest video games, often staying up late into the night working on his next big project.

Lily, on the other hand, was the curious explorer. With her dark brown eyes, stylish glasses, and insatiable curiosity for puzzles, she always saw the world as one big adventure waiting to be discovered. She loved reading mystery novels, solving brain teasers, and exploring new places, even if those places were just the forgotten corners of her small town. She had a knack for noticing details that others overlooked, and her imagination often ran wild with possibilities.

One sunny afternoon, Max and Lily found themselves in Max's attic, a treasure trove of old family relics and forgotten memories. They were on a mission to find something interesting for their next school project. Dust motes danced in the beams of sunlight filtering through the small attic window as they sifted through old photo albums, stacks of books, and various antiques. The wooden beams of the attic creaked under their feet, and the air was thick with the scent of aged paper and forgotten stories.

"Hey, look at this!" Max exclaimed, holding up an ancient-looking computer covered in dust. It was an old desktop model, bulky and outdated compared to the sleek tablets and smartphones they were used to. The beige casing was yellowed with age, and the monitor was a clunky, boxy shape that made Lily giggle.

"What do you think it is?" Lily asked, brushing a strand of hair out of her face as she leaned in to get a closer look. Her glasses slid down her nose slightly, and she pushed them back up with a thoughtful expression. She loved the idea of uncovering secrets from the past, and this old computer seemed like a potential goldmine of history.

"I don't know, but I bet it still works," Max said with a grin. He loved a good challenge, and the thought of reviving an old computer was too tempting to pass up. His mind was already racing with possibilities of what they might find on it. Old games? Forgotten documents? Maybe even a secret diary from a relative?

As they examined the old computer, Lily's eyes caught a glint of something shiny wedged between the cables and manuals. She reached in and pulled out a small, mysterious

USB drive labeled "Cryptoverse" in faded, handwritten letters. The label was peeling at the edges, and the handwriting looked hurried and almost frantic.

"What do you think is on it?" Lily asked, her curiosity piqued. She turned the USB drive over in her hands, feeling the weight of mystery it seemed to carry. The word "Cryptoverse" sounded intriguing and futuristic, sparking her imagination even further.

"Only one way to find out," Max replied, already planning to plug it into his laptop downstairs. He was always eager to dive into the unknown, and this USB drive was no exception. He could feel the excitement bubbling up inside him, a familiar rush he got whenever he was about to discover something new.

They hurried down the narrow, creaky attic stairs, excitement bubbling inside them. Max's room was a perfect reflection of his personality, with posters of robots and video game characters on the walls, shelves overflowing with gadgets, and a desk cluttered with various electronics projects. He cleared a space on his cluttered desk, pushing aside wires, circuit boards, and half-finished projects. The room was dimly lit by the glow of multiple computer screens, casting an almost magical light on their faces as they prepared for their discovery.

Max powered up his laptop, the familiar hum of the machine adding to the anticipation. With a shared glance of excitement, they inserted the USB drive. The screen flickered, displaying a series of strange codes and symbols before a swirling vortex of colors appeared. Max and Lily exchanged a surprised look as the room around them seemed to dissolve into pixels. Before they could react, they were pulled into the screen, tumbling through a tunnel of lights and sounds.

When the world stopped spinning, Max and Lily found themselves standing in a completely different place. They were no longer in Max's room but in a dazzling digital landscape, filled with neon lights and futuristic buildings. The sky was a shimmering blend of blues and purples, and the air buzzed with the sound of data streams flowing like rivers. The ground beneath their feet was a grid of glowing lines, each step they took sending ripples through the digital terrain.

"Welcome to the Cryptoverse!" a cheerful voice greeted them. They turned to see a friendly-looking AI figure floating beside them, its body made of shifting codes and symbols. It had a holographic face that displayed a warm, welcoming smile. The AI's presence felt both comforting and awe-inspiring, like they had stepped into a world where anything was possible.

"I am Crypton, your guide in this digital world. Here, you will embark on a journey to learn about the fascinating world of cryptocurrency," Crypton explained with a smile. Its voice was smooth and reassuring, filled with a kind of wisdom that made Max and Lily feel like they were in good hands.

Max and Lily looked at each other, eyes wide with excitement and curiosity. This was going to be the adventure of a lifetime. Little did they know that their journey into the Cryptoverse would not only be full of thrilling challenges and puzzles but would also teach them invaluable lessons about the future of money and technology. They could hardly contain their excitement as they prepared to follow Crypton deeper into this mesmerizing new world, ready to uncover the secrets of cryptocurrency and embark on an unforgettable adventure.

CHAPTER 1: INTO THE CRYPTOVERSE

Max and Lily stood in awe as they took in the dazzling digital landscape of the Cryptoverse. The neon lights flickered and glowed in vibrant hues of blue, pink, and green. Tall, futuristic buildings surrounded them, their surfaces covered in shifting patterns of light and data. It felt as if they had stepped into a city from a science fiction movie.

The sky above was a mesmerizing blend of blues and purples, with streams of data flowing like rivers through the air. Everything seemed to be made of light and information. The ground beneath their feet was a grid of glowing lines, each step they took sending ripples through the digital terrain.

"This place is amazing," Lily said, her dark brown eyes wide with wonder behind her stylish glasses. She spun around, taking in the sights and sounds of the Cryptoverse. "It's like we're inside a video game."

"Yeah, it's incredible," Max replied, adjusting his headband and glasses. He could feel the excitement bubbling up inside him. "I wonder how all of this works."

Crypton, the friendly AI guide, floated beside them, its body made of shifting codes and symbols. Its holographic face displayed a warm, welcoming smile.

"As I mentioned before, the Cryptoverse is built on blockchain technology," Crypton said. "A blockchain is a digital ledger that records all transactions made with a particular cryptocurrency. It's like a public record that anyone can see, but it's secured using complex mathematical algorithms to ensure its integrity and security."

As Crypton spoke, a holographic display appeared in front of them, showing a visual representation of a blockchain. It looked like a chain of interconnected blocks, each one containing a list of transactions. The blocks glowed with a soft, pulsing light, and lines of code scrolled across their surfaces.

"Each block in the chain contains a list of transactions," Crypton continued. "Once a block is added to the chain, it cannot be changed or removed. This makes the blockchain a secure and reliable way to record transactions."

Lily's eyes sparkled with curiosity. "So, it's like a digital ledger that everyone can see, but no one can tamper with?"

"Exactly," Crypton replied with a smile. "The blockchain is decentralized, meaning that it is not controlled by any single entity. Instead, it is maintained by a network of computers all around the world. This ensures that the blockchain remains secure and transparent."

Max and Lily nodded, their minds racing with new information. They could see that the Cryptoverse was a complex and fascinating place, filled with endless possibilities.

"Follow me," Crypton said, floating ahead of them. "There's much more to see and learn."

As they walked through the vibrant streets of the Cryptoverse, they saw holographic billboards displaying real-time updates of cryptocurrency prices. Avatars of people from all over the world interacted in bustling virtual marketplaces, trading goods and services using various cryptocurrencies. The ground beneath their feet continued to pulse with light, guiding their way through this incredible new world.

"Cryptocurrency is a digital or virtual form of money that uses cryptography for security," Crypton explained as they walked. "Unlike traditional money issued by governments, cryptocurrencies are decentralized and operate on the blockchain."

Max and Lily watched as a group of avatars gathered around a large holographic display, participating in what appeared to be a digital auction. The auctioneer's voice echoed through the air, and the avatars raised their hands to place bids using their digital wallets.

"Cryptocurrencies can be used for a wide range of transactions," Crypton said. "From buying goods and services to investing and trading. The possibilities are endless."

They continued to explore, passing through various districts of the Cryptoverse. Each district had its own unique theme and atmosphere, showcasing the diverse ways in which blockchain technology and cryptocurrencies could be used.

In one district, they saw a vibrant marketplace where artists were selling digital artworks as NFTs (non-fungible tokens). The artworks were displayed as holograms, each one unique and authenticated by the blockchain. Max and Lily were fascinated by the creativity and innovation on display.

"This is incredible," Lily said, her eyes wide with wonder. "I never realized how much you could do with cryptocurrency."

"Indeed," Crypton replied. "The Cryptoverse is a place where innovation and imagination come together. There are endless possibilities for those who are willing to explore and learn."

As they walked, Max and Lily continued to ask questions and learn more about the Cryptoverse. They learned about the importance of digital wallets, which allowed them to store, send, and receive cryptocurrency securely. Crypton explained how transactions were verified by the network of computers maintaining the blockchain, ensuring that every transaction was legitimate and secure.

Max and Lily were also introduced to the concept of mining, where powerful computers solved complex mathematical problems to add new blocks to the blockchain. In return for their work, miners were rewarded with new cryptocurrency tokens. It was a fascinating process that showed the intricate balance of security and reward within the blockchain.

By the time they reached the end of their tour, Max and Lily were bursting with new knowledge and excitement. They felt like they had only scratched the surface of what the Cryptoverse had to offer, and they were eager to learn more.

"Thank you, Crypton," Max said, adjusting his headband with a determined look. "This has been amazing."

"You're welcome," Crypton replied with a smile. "Your journey in the Cryptoverse has just begun. There is much more to learn and discover, and I will be here to guide you every step of the way."

As they stood in the heart of the Cryptoverse, surrounded by the vibrant, pulsing energy of the digital world, Max and Lily felt a sense of wonder and excitement. They knew that they were about to embark on an adventure unlike any other, one that would take them deep into the fascinating world of cryptocurrency and blockchain technology. And with Crypton by their side, they were ready to face whatever challenges and discoveries lay ahead.

CHAPTER 2: DIGITAL MYSTERIES

Max and Lily, still buzzing with excitement from their initial exploration of the Cryptoverse, followed Crypton through the vibrant streets. The digital landscape continued to astonish them, with its blend of futuristic architecture and mesmerizing light displays. The avatars around them moved with purpose, each engaged in their own unique activities, from trading digital assets to discussing technological innovations.

Crypton led them to a grand building labeled "Crypto Central." The structure was a marvel of digital engineering, its exterior made of shimmering holographic panels that reflected the ever-changing data streams. As they stepped inside, they were greeted by a spacious atrium filled with interactive exhibits and displays.

"Welcome to Crypto Central," Crypton said. "This is where you'll learn more about the core concepts of cryptocurrency. Let's start with digital wallets."

Max and Lily approached a large interactive screen that displayed various types of digital wallets. Crypton explained,

"A digital wallet is like a magical pouch that allows you to store, send, and receive cryptocurrency. It's secure and only accessible by you."

As they listened, a holographic display of a digital wallet appeared, showing its various components. "Software wallets are apps you can install on your computer or smartphone," Crypton continued. "They're convenient and easy to use, but you need to secure them with strong passwords and two-factor authentication."

"Hardware wallets are physical devices that store your cryptocurrency offline," Crypton said, showing an image of a sleek, USB-like device. "They're safer because they're not connected to the internet, making them less likely to get hacked."

"And paper wallets?" Lily asked, intrigued.

"A paper wallet is a physical printout of your public and private keys," Crypton explained, displaying a piece of paper with QR codes. "It's a secure way to store your cryptocurrency offline, but you need to keep it safe from damage or loss."

Max and Lily nodded, absorbing the information. "So, what's the difference between a public key and a private key?" Max asked.

"Think of your public key as your digital address," Crypton replied. "It's like your home address, which you can share with others so they can send you cryptocurrency. Your private key, on the other hand, is like the key to your house.

It lets you access your wallet and send cryptocurrency. Never share your private key with anyone."

As they continued their tour, Crypton led them to an exhibit showcasing various cryptocurrencies. "There are many different cryptocurrencies, each with its own unique features," Crypton said. "Bitcoin was the first cryptocurrency, created in 2009. It's like digital gold because it's valuable and there's a limited amount of it."

A holographic Bitcoin floated in front of them, its golden surface gleaming with digital light. "Bitcoin is not controlled by any single person or company," Crypton explained. "Transactions are verified by many computers around the world, making it secure and transparent."

Next, Crypton showed them Ethereum, represented by a sleek, silver hologram. "Ethereum is more than just a currency," Crypton said. "It's a platform where people can create smart contracts and apps. Smart contracts are like digital agreements that automatically execute when certain conditions are met."

Max's eyes lit up with interest. "So, Ethereum can be used to create all sorts of applications?"

"Exactly," Crypton replied. "From finance apps to games, Ethereum has a wide range of uses."

As they moved through the exhibits, Crypton introduced them to other notable cryptocurrencies like Litecoin, known for its faster transaction times, and Ripple, designed for quick and easy international payments. Each cryptocurrency had its own story and purpose, adding to the rich tapestry of the Cryptoverse.

After learning about the various cryptocurrencies, Crypton led them to a quieter area where they could sit and discuss what they had learned. The room was cozy, with comfortable chairs and holographic screens displaying calming scenes of nature.

"You've learned a lot today," Crypton said, its voice gentle and encouraging. "Now it's time to give you your own digital wallets and some crypto tokens to use on your journey."

Max and Lily followed Crypton's instructions, creating their own digital wallets on their devices. The process was straightforward, and soon they were looking at the balance of their new crypto tokens displayed on their screens.

"These tokens are your gateway to interacting with the Cryptoverse," Crypton explained. "Think of them as magical coins that can be used for a variety of purposes, from buying goods and services to participating in exciting adventures."

Max and Lily exchanged excited glances. They felt like they were part of something truly special, a world where technology and imagination came together in ways they had never thought possible.

As they stood up to leave, Crypton gave them a final piece of advice. "Remember, the Cryptoverse is a place of endless possibilities, but it's also important to stay safe and secure.

Protect your private keys, and always be cautious when making transactions."

Max and Lily nodded, taking Crypton's words to heart as they stepped out of Crypto Central. The bustling digital marketplace was alive with activity, and they felt a renewed sense of excitement as they prepared to continue their journey.

As they made their way through the crowd, a tall figure with a friendly smile and sharp, digital suit approached them. He had slicked-back hair, gleaming eyes, and a confident demeanor. A holographic badge floated beside him, displaying the name "Elias."

"Hello there, young explorers!" Elias greeted them warmly. "I couldn't help but notice your enthusiasm for learning about the Cryptoverse. I'm Elias, and I have a special offer just for you."

Max and Lily exchanged curious glances. "What kind of offer?" Max asked, intrigued.

Elias leaned in slightly, lowering his voice as if sharing a secret. "How would you like to receive some free Ethereum? All you need to do is send me a small amount of Ethereum first, and I'll send you back double the amount. It's a promotion to help new users get started in the Cryptoverse."

Max's eyes widened with excitement. "That sounds amazing! What do you think, Lily?"

Lily hesitated, her dark brown eyes narrowing thoughtfully

behind her stylish glasses. Something about the offer didn't sit right with her. She had always been good at spotting inconsistencies and had a keen sense for when things seemed too good to be true.

"Wait a minute," Lily said, turning to Elias. "Why do we have to send you Ethereum first? If it's a promotion, shouldn't you just give us the free Ethereum directly?"

Elias's smile faltered for a brief moment before he quickly regained his composure. "Ah, well, it's just a way to confirm that you have an active wallet and are ready to receive the funds. It's a standard procedure."

Max looked at Lily, uncertainty clouding his features. "What do you think? Should we do it?"

Lily shook her head slowly. "No, Max. I don't think we should. It doesn't make sense to have to send Ethereum first to get more in return. It feels like a trap."

Max paused, considering Lily's words. He trusted her instincts and knew she had a knack for seeing through tricks and puzzles. "You're right, Lily. It does sound fishy. We shouldn't do it."

Elias's smile faded entirely, replaced by a look of annoyance. "Fine, suit yourselves," he said curtly before disappearing into the crowd.

Crypton, who had been observing from a distance, floated over with a proud expression. "Well done, Max and Lily. You passed the security test."

"A test?" Max echoed, surprised.

"Yes," Crypton confirmed. "What Elias offered you is a common scam in the cryptocurrency space. Scammers often promise free cryptocurrency in exchange for a small payment upfront, but once you send them your funds, they disappear, and you never receive anything in return. It's important to be vigilant and question offers that seem too good to be true."

Lily smiled, feeling a sense of accomplishment. "I'm glad we trusted our instincts."

"Always trust your instincts and be cautious," Crypton advised. "The Cryptoverse is full of opportunities, but it's also important to stay safe and protect your assets. You've both shown great wisdom today."

Max and Lily thanked Crypton, their excitement undiminished but tempered with a newfound sense of caution. They continued their journey through the Cryptoverse, ready to face whatever challenges and discoveries lay ahead, knowing that they had the knowledge and instincts to navigate this incredible digital world safely.

CHAPTER 3: THE FIRST CHALLENGE

Max and Lily continued their exploration of the Cryptoverse, their excitement tempered with a sense of vigilance after their encounter with Elias. The bustling streets and vibrant marketplaces were filled with endless possibilities, but they knew they had to stay alert. They felt like adventurers in a new and wondrous land, ready to face whatever challenges lay ahead.

Crypton led them to a quiet courtyard filled with lush digital trees that shimmered with vibrant colors. The air was cool and filled with the soft hum of data streams. As they settled onto a bench, Crypton's expression grew serious.

"Max, Lily," Crypton began, "there's something important I need to tell you. The Cryptoverse is in danger."

Max and Lily exchanged worried glances. "What kind of danger?" Max asked, leaning forward.

Crypton conjured a holographic image of a menacing figure. The figure was cloaked in shadows, with glowing red eyes and jagged lines of code running across its form.

"This is Hackzor, a malicious virus that seeks to corrupt the blockchain and steal people's tokens. Hackzor is cunning and dangerous, and if he succeeds, it could cause chaos and ruin the Cryptoverse."

Lily's eyes widened behind her stylish glasses. "But why does he want to do that?"

Crypton sighed. "Hackzor was once a brilliant programmer who became obsessed with power and control. He was known as Dr. Hex, a genius in the world of digital security. But over time, his obsession grew, and he became convinced that the decentralized nature of the Cryptoverse was chaotic and needed to be brought under a single, powerful ruler—himself."

Crypton continued, "Dr. Hex believed that by corrupting the blockchain, he could manipulate the entire Cryptoverse to his will, stealing tokens and wreaking havoc. He transformed himself into Hackzor, a virus that could infiltrate and corrupt the very fabric of the digital world. He thrives on chaos and wants to bring everything under his dark influence."

Max clenched his fists. "We can't let that happen. What can we do to stop him?"

Crypton nodded. "To stop Hackzor, you need to find the Four Crypto Keys. These keys are powerful artifacts scattered across different regions of the Cryptoverse. Each key holds the power to secure a part of the blockchain. Together, they can restore security and peace."

Lily's curiosity was piqued. "Where do we find these keys?"

Crypton projected a map of the Cryptoverse, highlighting four distinct regions: the Mining Mountains, the Smart Contract City, the NFT Forest, and the DeFi Dungeon. Each region was marked with a glowing symbol representing a Crypto Key.

"Your first destination is the Mining Mountains," Crypton explained. "There, you will learn about the process of mining and how new tokens are created. But be warned, Hackzor's minions may be lurking, trying to stop you."

Max and Lily felt a mix of excitement and determination. They were ready to face whatever challenges lay ahead to save the Cryptoverse from Hackzor's evil plans.

Crypton led them to a shimmering portal at the edge of the courtyard. "This portal will take you to the Mining Mountains," Crypton said. "But there's one more thing you need to know. To travel through the portal and move around the Cryptoverse, you'll need to pay a gas fee."

"A gas fee?" Max asked, puzzled.

"Yes," Crypton replied. "A gas fee is a small amount of cryptocurrency that you pay to perform transactions on the blockchain. It's like paying for fuel to power your journey. The fee goes to the miners who work to process and verify your transaction, ensuring it gets added to the blockchain."

Lily nodded, understanding. "So, it's like paying a toll to use a special road?"

"Exactly," Crypton said. "Now, you can use your digital wallets to pay the gas fee and activate the portal."

Max and Lily opened their digital wallets and followed Crypton's instructions to pay the gas fee. The process was simple, and they watched as a small amount of their cryptocurrency was deducted and the portal began to glow brighter.

"Are you ready?" Max asked, holding out his hand to Lily.

Lily nodded, gripping his hand firmly. "Ready."

They stepped into the portal together, feeling a rush of energy as they were transported across the Cryptoverse. The journey through the portal was like a rollercoaster ride, with vibrant colors and lights whizzing past them. They felt weightless, as if they were floating through a tunnel of pure energy.

After what felt like both an instant and an eternity, they emerged from the portal and found themselves standing at the foot of the Mining Mountains. The mountains were a breathtaking sight, with towering peaks made of shimmering digital minerals. The air was filled with the rhythmic sound of mining machines and the distant chatter of miners.

"Welcome to the Mining Mountains," Crypton said, appearing beside them. "Your journey begins here. Be vigilant, stay together, and remember the lessons you've learned. The fate of the Cryptoverse rests in your hands."

Max and Lily took a deep breath, looking at the majestic

mountains before them. They knew this was just the beginning of a grand adventure. Holding the Crypto Compass tightly, they set off on the path that would lead them to their first Crypto Key, ready to uncover the mysteries of the Mining Mountains.

As they ventured deeper into the mountains, they couldn't help but wonder what other secrets and challenges awaited them in the Cryptoverse.

CHAPTER 4: THE MINING MOUNTAINS

Max and Lily stood at the base of the Mining Mountains, their eyes wide with wonder as they took in the dazzling peaks of shimmering digital minerals. The mountains seemed to hum with energy, and the air was filled with the rhythmic sound of mining machines and the distant chatter of miners.

"This place is incredible," Max said, adjusting his headband and glasses. "I can't wait to see how mining works."

"Me too," Lily agreed, her dark brown eyes sparkling with curiosity behind her stylish glasses. "Let's find out more about it."

Crypton, their friendly AI guide, floated beside them, its holographic face beaming with pride. "Welcome to the Mining Mountains," Crypton said. "This is where new cryptocurrency tokens are created through a process called mining. Miners use powerful computers to solve complex puzzles, and when they solve a puzzle, they add a new block to the blockchain and are rewarded with new tokens."

As they walked along the path, they saw miners hard at

work, using advanced machinery to extract digital minerals from the mountain walls. The ground beneath their feet was a grid of glowing lines, and each step they took sent ripples through the digital terrain.

"Look, there's someone who can help us," Lily said, pointing to a robust figure with a friendly smile and strong arms. He wore a helmet with a headlamp that cast a warm glow in the dimly lit tunnels of the mountain.

"Hello there! I'm Min," the miner character greeted them, extending a hand. "Crypton told me you'd be coming. I'm here to help you understand mining and find the first Crypto Key."

Max and Lily shook Min's hand, eager to learn and start their quest. "Nice to meet you, Min. We're ready to learn and find the key," Max said.

Min led them deeper into the tunnels, the walls glittering with veins of digital minerals. The air was cool and filled with the hum of mining machines. "Mining is the process by which new cryptocurrency tokens are created," Min explained. "Miners use powerful computers to solve complex mathematical puzzles. When they solve a puzzle, they add a new block to the blockchain and are rewarded with new tokens."

"So, mining helps keep the blockchain secure?" Lily asked, intrigued.

"Exactly," Min said with a nod. "The puzzles are so difficult that it takes a lot of computational power to solve them, which makes it hard for anyone to tamper with the blockchain."

Max watched in fascination as a miner's machine solved a puzzle, and a block of glowing tokens appeared on the screen. "It's like a giant treasure hunt, but instead of finding gold, you create new tokens," Max remarked.

Min smiled. "That's one way to think about it. Now, to find the first Crypto Key, you'll need to solve a series of puzzles and overcome a few obstacles. But don't worry, I'll be here to guide you."

They reached a large cavern filled with mining machines and holographic displays. In the center of the cavern was a giant, intricate puzzle made of glowing blocks. "This is your first challenge," Min said. "You need to arrange the blocks in the correct order to unlock the passage to the key."

Max and Lily examined the puzzle, their minds racing with possibilities. "Let's think this through," Lily said, studying the blocks carefully. "Each block has a different pattern. We need to match the patterns to form a complete sequence."

Max nodded, his fingers already working on rearranging the blocks. "I'll start with this block. It looks like it could be the beginning of the sequence."

Together, they worked on the puzzle, their teamwork and problem-solving skills complementing each other perfectly. After a few minutes of intense concentration, they successfully arranged the blocks, and the passageway opened with a soft glow.

"Great job!" Min cheered. "You're one step closer to the Crypto Key. Now, follow me."

They continued through the tunnels, facing various challenges that tested their knowledge of blockchain and cryptocurrency. In one section, they had to solve riddles that required them to understand how transactions were verified and added to the blockchain. In another, they had to navigate a maze filled with traps set by Hackzor's minions.

Max and Lily's determination never wavered, and they overcame each obstacle with skill and ingenuity. Finally, they reached a hidden chamber deep within the mountain. In the center of the chamber, glowing with a bright, ethereal light, was the first Crypto Key.

Max reached out and took the key, feeling a surge of energy as it connected to his digital wallet. "We did it!" he exclaimed, turning to Lily with a triumphant smile.

Lily grinned back. "One down, three to go."

Crypton appeared beside them, its face beaming with pride. "Well done, Max and Lily. You've successfully recovered the first Crypto Key. This key will help secure a part of the blockchain and protect it from Hackzor's corruption."

"What's next?" Max asked, eager to continue their adventure.

"Your next destination is the Smart Contract City," Crypton said. "There, you'll learn about smart contracts and find the second Crypto Key."

As they prepared to leave the Mining Mountains, Min handed them a small token. "Take this with you. It will help you on your journey and remind you of what you've accomplished here."

Max and Lily thanked Min and Crypton, their hearts filled with a sense of achievement and excitement for what lay ahead. They stepped back through the portal, ready to face the challenges and discoveries that awaited them in the Smart Contract City.

With the first Crypto Key in hand and their spirits high, Max and Lily knew they were on the right path to saving the Cryptoverse from Hackzor's evil plans. And as they ventured into the next chapter of their adventure, they felt more determined than ever to uncover the secrets of the digital world and protect it from harm.

CHAPTER 5: THE SMART CONTRACT CITY

Max and Lily emerged from the portal and found themselves standing at the entrance of the Smart Contract City. The city was a marvel of futuristic architecture, with tall, sleek buildings made of shimmering glass and holographic displays. Neon lights danced along the streets, and digital billboards showcased various smart contract applications in action. The air buzzed with energy, and the atmosphere was alive with the hum of innovation.

"Welcome to the Smart Contract City," Crypton said, appearing beside them. "This is a place where digital agreements, called smart contracts, are made. Smart contracts are self-executing agreements with the terms of the contract directly written into code. They automatically execute when the conditions are met, eliminating the need for intermediaries."

Max and Lily looked around in awe, taking in the bustling activity of the city. Avatars moved with purpose, interacting with holographic interfaces and engaging in lively discussions about their projects.

"This place is incredible," Lily said, her dark brown eyes wide with wonder behind her stylish glasses. "I can't wait to learn more about smart contracts."

"Let's find someone who can help us," Max suggested, adjusting his headband and glasses.

As they walked through the city, they noticed a large crowd gathered around a holographic display in the center of a plaza. Curious, they approached the crowd and saw a tall, elegant figure explaining something to the gathered avatars. The figure had a kind smile and an air of confidence, with a holographic badge displaying the name "Sophy."

"Hello, everyone. I'm Sophy, a smart contract expert," she said warmly. "Today, I'll be demonstrating how smart contracts work and how they can be used to resolve disputes."

Max and Lily exchanged excited glances. This was exactly what they needed.

After the demonstration, they approached Sophy. "Excuse us, Sophy," Lily began, "we're on a quest to find the Crypto Keys and save the Cryptoverse from Hackzor. Crypton told us that you could help us understand smart contracts."

Sophy's eyes lit up with interest. "Of course, I'd be happy to help. Smart contracts are a powerful tool in the Cryptoverse. Let's start with the basics."

Sophy led them to a quiet corner of the plaza, where a holographic display appeared, showing the inner workings of a smart contract. "A smart contract is like a digital agreement that automatically enforces the terms of the contract. It's written in code and runs on the blockchain, making it secure and transparent."

"Can you give us an example that kids our age would understand?" Max asked, intrigued.

"Sure," Sophy replied. "Imagine you and your friends want to create a simple game. You all agree that the winner will get a prize. You can use a smart contract to make sure everyone sticks to the agreement."

Max and Lily nodded, eager to hear more.

Sophy continued, "Let's say the game is a race. The smart contract would include the names of all the players and the rules of the race. When the race is over, the smart contract automatically checks who the winner is. If Max wins, the contract will transfer the prize to his digital wallet. If Lily wins, the prize goes to her. This way, no one can cheat, and the prize is given fairly."

Lily's eyes sparkled with understanding. "So, it's like having a referee that makes sure everyone plays by the rules and gets their prize."

"Exactly," Sophy said with a smile. "And because the smart contract runs on the blockchain, everyone can see that the rules were followed, and no one can change the outcome."

As they continued their conversation, an avatar approached them, looking distressed. "Excuse me, are you Sophy?" the avatar asked.

"Yes, I am," Sophy replied. "How can I help you?"

"I'm having a dispute with my business partner," the avatar explained. "We agreed to split the profits from our project equally, but now he's refusing to honor our agreement. Can you help us resolve this using a smart contract?"

Sophy nodded. "Of course. Let's gather the details and create a smart contract to settle the dispute."

The avatar provided the necessary information, and Sophy began writing the smart contract. She explained each step to Max and Lily, showing them how the contract was coded to enforce the terms of the agreement.

"First, we define the parties involved," Sophy said, highlighting the relevant lines of code. "Then, we specify the conditions under which the tokens will be transferred. In this case, the contract will split the profits equally between the two partners once the project is completed."

Once the smart contract was written, Sophy deployed it on the blockchain. The business partner, who had been watching from a distance, reluctantly agreed to the terms. The smart contract executed flawlessly, and the profits were split equally between the two partners.

"Thank you, Sophy," the avatar said, relieved. "You've saved my business."

"You're welcome," Sophy replied. "That's the power of smart contracts. They ensure that agreements are honored and disputes are resolved fairly."

Max and Lily were impressed by how smart contracts worked and the practical examples they had seen. "This is amazing," Max said. "Smart contracts can solve so many problems."

"Indeed," Sophy said. "And now, it's time for you to find the second Crypto Key. To do that, you'll need to create and execute a smart contract successfully."

Sophy led them to a large, ornate door at the edge of the plaza. "Behind this door is a challenge that will test your understanding of smart contracts. Complete the challenge, and the Crypto Key will be yours."

Max and Lily nodded, their determination renewed. They stepped through the door and found themselves in a grand hall filled with holographic displays and intricate puzzles. At the center of the hall was a large pedestal with a glowing crystal atop it.

A voice echoed through the hall, explaining the challenge. "To unlock the second Crypto Key, you must create a smart contract that ensures the crystal is transferred to you once you solve the puzzles. Work together and use what you've learned."

Max and Lily set to work, examining the puzzles and discussing how to write the smart contract. They coded the contract to recognize when the puzzles were solved and to transfer the crystal to them upon completion.

With careful teamwork and problem-solving, they solved

the puzzles one by one. As they completed the final puzzle, the smart contract activated, and the crystal floated down from the pedestal, transforming into the second Crypto Key.

"We did it!" Max exclaimed, holding the key triumphantly.

Lily grinned. "We couldn't have done it without the smart contract."

Crypton appeared beside them, beaming with pride. "Well done, Max and Lily. You've successfully used a smart contract to unlock the second Crypto Key. This key will help secure another part of the blockchain and protect it from Hackzor's corruption."

"What's next?" Max asked, eager to continue their adventure.

"Your next destination is the NFT Forest," Crypton said. "There, you'll learn about non-fungible tokens and find the third Crypto Key."

As they prepared to leave the Smart Contract City, Sophy handed them a small token. "Take this with you. It will help you on your journey and remind you of what you've accomplished here."

Max and Lily thanked Sophy and Crypton, their hearts filled with a sense of achievement and excitement for what lay ahead. They stepped back through the portal, ready to face the challenges and discoveries that awaited them in the NFT Forest.

With the second Crypto Key in hand and their spirits high,

Max and Lily knew they were on the right path to saving the Cryptoverse from Hackzor's evil plans. And as they ventured into the next chapter of their adventure, they felt more determined than ever to uncover the secrets of the digital world and protect it from harm.

CHAPTER 6: THE NFT FOREST

Max and Lily emerged from the portal and found themselves standing at the edge of the NFT Forest. The forest was unlike anything they had seen before, a vibrant digital landscape filled with towering trees made of glowing pixels and leaves that shimmered with all the colors of the rainbow. The air was filled with the soft rustle of digital leaves and the occasional chirp of holographic birds.

"Welcome to the NFT Forest," Crypton said, appearing beside them. "This is where unique digital items, known as NFTs or non-fungible tokens, are created and traded. Each NFT is one-of-a-kind and can represent anything from art to music to collectibles."

Max and Lily looked around in awe. The forest was teeming with activity, with avatars moving through the trees, examining digital artworks, and engaging in animated discussions about their latest creations.

"This place is amazing," Lily said, her dark brown eyes wide with wonder behind her stylish glasses. "I can't wait to learn more about NFTs."

"Let's find someone who can help us," Max suggested, adjusting his headband and glasses.

As they walked through the forest, they noticed a group of avatars gathered around a clearing where a tall, eccentric figure was working on a holographic canvas. The figure had wild, colorful hair and wore an artist's smock splattered with virtual paint. A holographic badge floated beside him, displaying the name "Artie."

"Hello, everyone! I'm Artie, an NFT artist," he said, not looking up from his work. "Today, I'm creating a new series of digital art pieces that will be turned into NFTs."

Max and Lily exchanged excited glances. This was exactly what they needed.

After watching Artie for a while, they approached him. "Excuse us, Artie," Max began, "we're on a quest to find the Crypto Keys and save the Cryptoverse from Hackzor. Crypton told us that you could help us understand NFTs."

Artie finally looked up, his eyes sparkling with enthusiasm. "Of course, I'd be delighted to help! NFTs are a wonderful way to express creativity and ownership in the digital world. Let's start with the basics."

Artie led them to a quiet grove filled with holographic displays showcasing various NFTs. "An NFT, or non-fungible token, is a unique digital item that you own. It's stored on the blockchain, which means everyone can see who owns it and that it can't be copied or altered."

Lily tilted her head, thinking. "So, how is owning an NFT different from, say, having a digital picture on your phone?"

"Great question!" Artie replied. "Think of it like collecting rare baseball cards, football cards, or Pokémon cards. Each card has value because it's unique and not everyone has it. NFTs work the same way. When you own an NFT, you own the original digital item, and that ownership is recorded on the blockchain for everyone to see."

Max's eyes lit up. "So, it's like having a rare card that everyone knows is yours and can't be copied?"

"Exactly," Artie said with a smile. "And because the ownership is on the blockchain, it's secure and transparent. Anyone can see who owns it, but no one can alter it or create a fake version."

As they continued their conversation, a group of avatars approached them, looking excited. "Artie, we heard about the NFT scavenger hunt! Can we join?" one of them asked.

Artie smiled broadly. "Of course! The scavenger hunt is a great way to explore the NFT Forest and learn about the value of digital ownership and creativity. Plus, there's a special prize for finding all the items – the third Crypto Key!"

Max and Lily's eyes lit up with excitement. "We definitely want to join," Max said.

"Great! Here's how it works," Artie explained. "I've hidden several unique NFTs around the forest. Each one represents a different aspect of digital creativity. Use the clues to find them all, and the final clue will lead you to the Crypto Key."

Artie handed them a small digital device that displayed the first clue: "Find the tree with leaves of gold, where stories of old are digitally told."

Max and Lily set off into the forest, their eyes scanning the surroundings for any sign of the golden leaves. As they walked, they marveled at the variety of digital artworks displayed on the trees and the ground.

"Look, over there!" Lily pointed to a tree with shimmering golden leaves. They approached it and found a holographic book nestled among the branches.

Max reached out and touched the book, and a new clue appeared on their device: "Seek the waterfall of colors bright, where music flows and pixels light."

They continued their journey, following the clues that led them through the vibrant forest. They discovered an NFT representing a piece of music at a cascading waterfall of colors and a virtual sculpture hidden in a grove of glowing trees. Each NFT they found was unique and beautiful, showcasing the endless possibilities of digital creativity.

Finally, the last clue led them to a secluded glen where a majestic holographic statue stood. The statue held a glowing key in its hand, and as Max and Lily approached, the key transformed into the third Crypto Key.

"We did it!" Max exclaimed, holding the key triumphantly.

Lily grinned. "The NFT scavenger hunt was amazing. We learned so much about digital ownership and creativity."

Crypton appeared beside them, beaming with pride. "Well done, Max and Lily. You've successfully completed the NFT scavenger hunt and earned the third Crypto Key. This key will help secure another part of the blockchain and protect it from Hackzor's corruption."

"What's next?" Max asked, eager to continue their adventure.

"Your final destination is the DeFi Dungeon," Crypton said. "There, you'll learn about decentralized finance and find the fourth Crypto Key."

Max and Lily thanked Artie and Crypton, their hearts filled with a sense of achievement and excitement for what lay ahead. They stepped back through the portal, ready to face the challenges and discoveries that awaited them in the DeFi Dungeon.

CHAPTER 7: THE DEFI DUNGEON

Max and Lily emerged from the portal and found themselves standing at the entrance of the DeFi Dungeon. The dungeon was a vast, underground labyrinth with walls made of shimmering digital blocks and pathways illuminated by flickering torches. The atmosphere was filled with an air of mystery and challenge, as if the very walls held secrets waiting to be uncovered.

"Welcome to the DeFi Dungeon," Crypton said, appearing beside them. "This is where you'll learn about decentralized finance, or DeFi. DeFi is a system of financial services that operates on the blockchain, allowing people to lend, borrow, and earn interest without the need for traditional banks."

Max and Lily exchanged intrigued glances. "This sounds different from everything we've learned so far," Max said, adjusting his headband and glasses.

"Let's find someone who can guide us," Lily suggested, her dark brown eyes shining with curiosity behind her stylish glasses.

As they ventured deeper into the dungeon, they came across a large chamber filled with glowing symbols and intricate machinery. In the center of the chamber stood a tall figure with a long, flowing robe and a staff that glowed with magical energy. The figure had a wise, kindly face and a holographic badge displaying the name "Finny."

"Greetings, travelers! I am Finny, the financial wizard," he said, his voice echoing through the chamber. "Crypton told me you would be coming. I am here to teach you about the wonders of decentralized finance."

Max and Lily approached Finny, eager to learn. "We're on a quest to find the Crypto Keys and save the Cryptoverse from Hackzor," Max explained. "We need to understand DeFi to complete our mission."

Finny smiled warmly. "You have come to the right place. DeFi is a powerful tool that empowers individuals to take control of their finances. Let's begin with the basics of lending and borrowing."

Finny led them to a series of holographic displays that showed how DeFi platforms operated. "In the traditional financial system, banks act as intermediaries, taking deposits from savers and lending them to borrowers. In DeFi, smart contracts on the blockchain handle these transactions, removing the need for banks."

Lily nodded, intrigued. "So, people can lend and borrow directly from each other?"

"Exactly," Finny replied. "For example, if you have extra cryptocurrency that you're not using, you can lend it out on a DeFi platform and earn interest. This is known as staking. On the other hand, if you need to borrow cryptocurrency, you can do so by providing collateral, which is something valuable you offer as a guarantee that you will repay the loan."

Max's eyes lit up. "So, staking is like putting your money in a savings account and earning interest?"

"Precisely," Finny said. "Interest is the extra money you earn when you lend your cryptocurrency. And because DeFi operates on the blockchain, it is transparent, secure, and accessible to anyone with an internet connection."

Finny then led them to another display showing a large pool of tokens. "This is a liquidity pool," he explained. "Liquidity pools are collections of cryptocurrency tokens that are locked in smart contracts. They provide liquidity, which means there are enough tokens available for users to trade without causing big changes in prices."

"Why is liquidity important?" Lily asked, curious.

"Liquidity ensures that people can buy and sell tokens easily," Finny said. "Without enough liquidity, it would be hard to trade tokens, and prices could become very unstable and change a lot, which is what we call volatile."

Max and Lily absorbed the information, understanding how these concepts were interconnected. Finny continued,

"Interest rates in DeFi are determined by supply and demand. Supply is how much of something is available, and demand is how much people want it. When more people want to borrow than lend, interest rates go up because the supply is lower than the demand. When more people are lending than borrowing, interest rates go down because the supply is higher than the demand."

"That makes sense," Max said. "So it's all about balancing the needs of borrowers and lenders."

"Exactly," Finny replied. "Now, to obtain the fourth and final Crypto Key, you must complete a DeFi challenge that uses these concepts. Are you ready?"

Max and Lily nodded, feeling a mix of excitement and determination. Finny led them to a large door adorned with intricate symbols of tokens and percentages. Beyond the door was a grand hall filled with holographic displays and complex machinery.

"In this challenge," Finny explained, "you need to use DeFi strategies to unlock the final key. You'll need to create a liquidity pool, manage interest rates, and provide collateral to complete the tasks. Let's begin with the first task: creating a liquidity pool."

Max and Lily approached a large holographic screen that displayed two different types of tokens. "To create a liquidity pool, you need to contribute equal amounts of two types of tokens," Finny instructed. "This helps provide liquidity for trading."

Max and Lily each selected a token and transferred equal amounts into the liquidity pool. The screen lit up with a successful message, and the first part of the challenge was complete.

"Great job!" Finny said. "Now, let's move on to managing interest rates. You'll need to adjust the interest rates based on supply and demand to ensure the system remains balanced."

They approached another screen that showed a graph of interest rates fluctuating based on borrowing and lending activity. Using what they had learned, Max and Lily adjusted the interest rates to balance the supply and demand, making sure there were enough lenders and borrowers in the system.

"Excellent work," Finny praised. "For the final task, you need to provide collateral to secure a loan. This demonstrates your understanding of how borrowing works in DeFi."

Max and Lily approached the final screen, where they were prompted to select a valuable item as collateral. They chose an NFT they had collected earlier in their journey. By providing this as collateral, they secured a loan, completing the last part of the challenge.

The room filled with a warm glow, and the fourth and final Crypto Key appeared on a pedestal. Max and Lily approached it, feeling a sense of accomplishment as they took the key.

"We did it!" Max exclaimed, holding the key triumphantly.

Lily grinned. "We've learned so much about decentralized finance and how it empowers people."

Crypton appeared beside them, beaming with pride. "Well done, Max and Lily. You've successfully completed the DeFi challenge and earned the fourth and final Crypto Key. This key will help secure the blockchain and protect it from Hackzor's corruption."

"What's next?" Max asked, eager to complete their mission.

"Now that you have all four Crypto Keys, you must head to the Core of the Cryptoverse," Crypton said. "There, you will use the keys to strengthen the blockchain and defeat Hackzor once and for all."

Max and Lily thanked Finny and Crypton, their hearts filled with a sense of achievement and excitement for the final challenge. They stepped back through the portal, ready to face the ultimate test and save the Cryptoverse from Hackzor's evil plans.

CHAPTER 8: THE FINAL SHOWDOWN

Max and Lily emerged from the portal and found themselves standing at the heart of the Cryptoverse, a place known as the Core. The Core was a vast, glowing chamber filled with intricate patterns of light and data streams that converged into a central node. The air hummed with energy, and the atmosphere was tense with anticipation.

"Welcome to the Core of the Cryptoverse," Crypton said, appearing beside them. "This is where the blockchain's central functions are managed. With the four Crypto Keys, you can restore security and defeat Hackzor once and for all."

Max and Lily exchanged determined glances. "We're ready," Max said, adjusting his headband and glasses.

Lily nodded, her dark brown eyes shining with resolve behind her stylish glasses. "Let's do this."

As they approached the central node, a menacing figure emerged from the shadows. Hackzor, with his cloaked form and glowing red eyes, stood before them, his presence exuding an aura of malevolence and power.

"You've come far, but this is where your journey ends," Hackzor sneered, his voice echoing through the chamber. "The Cryptoverse will be mine, and there's nothing you can do to stop me."

Max and Lily stood their ground, holding the four Crypto Keys tightly. "You're wrong, Hackzor," Max said firmly. "We've learned a lot about cryptocurrency and decentralized finance, and we're not going to let you corrupt the Cryptoverse."

Hackzor laughed darkly. "Very well. Let's see if your knowledge can save you."

With a wave of his hand, Hackzor unleashed a barrage of corrupted data streams aimed at Max and Lily. But they were ready. Using their understanding of blockchain security, they deflected the attacks by creating secure barriers of code, preventing Hackzor's corruption from reaching the Core.

"We need to use the Crypto Keys to stabilize the blockchain!" Lily shouted over the noise of the battle.

Max nodded, and together they approached the central node. They placed each key into its corresponding slot, and the room began to pulse with energy. The data streams around them grew brighter and more stable as the keys activated the security protocols.

Hackzor roared in anger. "No! This can't be happening!"

With the Crypto Keys in place, Max and Lily turned to face Hackzor. "It's over, Hackzor," Max said. "We understand how cryptocurrency works, and we're going to outsmart you."

Lily stepped forward, her voice strong and confident. "Cryptocurrency is built on trust and transparency. You thrive on chaos and deception, but we know how to protect the blockchain."

Using their knowledge of decentralized finance, they initiated a series of smart contracts that isolated Hackzor's corrupt code. These smart contracts acted as traps, binding Hackzor in a web of secure code that he couldn't escape.

"No! You can't do this to me!" Hackzor screamed, his form flickering as the smart contracts tightened around him.

Max and Lily watched as Hackzor's corrupted data streams were absorbed into the blockchain's security protocols. With a final roar, Hackzor was pulled into a digital jail cell made entirely of smart contracts, the bars glowing with a bright, unbreakable light.

The room grew quiet as the last remnants of Hackzor's power were contained within the smart contract jail cell. The data streams around them stabilized completely, and the Core glowed with a brilliant light.

Crypton appeared beside them, his face beaming with pride. "You did it, Max and Lily. You've defeated Hackzor and restored security to the Cryptoverse."

Max and Lily felt a wave of relief and triumph wash over them.

They had succeeded in their mission, and the Cryptoverse was safe once again.

"As a reward for your bravery and knowledge, I present you with a special token," Crypton said, holding out a glowing, intricately designed token. "This token will allow you to return to the Cryptoverse anytime you wish."

Max took the token, marveling at its beauty. "Thank you, Crypton. We couldn't have done it without your guidance."

Lily smiled. "We'll make sure to use what we've learned to help others and continue exploring the possibilities of the Cryptoverse."

Crypton nodded. "You have proven yourselves to be true champions of the Cryptoverse. Your knowledge and courage have made a lasting impact."

As they prepared to leave, Max looked back at the smart contract jail cell where Hackzor was contained. "What will happen to Hackzor?"

Crypton's expression grew serious. "He is trapped within the smart contract jail cell, but we must remain vigilant. The Cryptoverse is always evolving, and we must be prepared for any future threats."

Max and Lily nodded, understanding the gravity of the situation. They activated the special token, and the room around them dissolved into a swirl of colors. They felt themselves being transported back to the real world.

When the world around them solidified, they found themselves back in Max's room, their computer screen displaying a message of congratulations from Crypton.

CHAPTER 9: BACK HOME

When the world around them solidified, Max and Lily found themselves back in Max's room, their computer screen displaying a message of congratulations from Crypton. The familiar surroundings felt comforting, but the experience they had just been through left them with a sense of newfound purpose.

"We're back," Max said, looking around with a smile. The digital adventures seemed like a dream, but the Crypto Keys in his hand were proof of their journey.

Lily adjusted her glasses, her eyes filled with excitement. "That was an incredible adventure. And now we can return anytime we want."

Max nodded, holding the special token tightly. "The Cryptoverse is safe, and we have the knowledge to continue exploring and protecting it."

As they sat down to catch their breath, Max's mother called from downstairs. "Max, Lily! Dinner's ready!"

They exchanged amused glances. "After everything we've been through, it's funny to think about something as normal as dinner," Max said with a chuckle.

Lily grinned. "Yeah, but it's nice to be home."

They made their way downstairs, where the aroma of freshly cooked food filled the air. Max's mom had prepared a delicious spread, and as they sat down, she noticed the excitement in their eyes.

"You two seem to be in good spirits. What have you been up to?" she asked.

Max and Lily exchanged a knowing look. "Oh, just exploring new worlds and saving the Cryptoverse," Max said playfully.

His mom laughed. "Well, whatever it is, it sounds like you had fun."

After dinner, Max and Lily sat in the backyard, discussing their adventure.

"We learned so much about cryptocurrency and how it works," Max said thoughtfully. "It's amazing how much there is to explore."

Lily nodded. "I think we should share what we've learned with others. There are probably a lot of kids who would find this just as exciting as we did."

Max's eyes lit up. "You're right. We could start a club—like a Crypto Kids Club—where we teach other kids about cryptocurrency and technology."

Lily's face brightened with enthusiasm. "That sounds awesome! We could have meetings, share what we learned, and maybe even do some fun projects."

The next day, they set their plan into motion. They created colorful flyers inviting kids from their school to join the Crypto Kids Club. The flyers promised exciting lessons on cryptocurrency, fun activities, and a chance to learn about the future of technology.

Max and Lily handed out the flyers at school, and the response was overwhelmingly positive. Kids were curious and excited about the idea of learning something new and cutting-edge.

Their first meeting was held in Max's garage, which they had transformed into a makeshift classroom with posters and charts explaining basic cryptocurrency concepts. Max stood in front of a whiteboard, while Lily prepared a laptop to show some interactive demonstrations.

"Welcome to the first meeting of the Crypto Kids Club!" Max began, his voice filled with enthusiasm. "We're excited to share what we've learned about the amazing world of cryptocurrency."

Lily took over, explaining the basics in a way that was easy for everyone to understand. "Cryptocurrency is like digital money. It works on a technology called blockchain, which is a secure way to record transactions. Today, we'll learn about how it works and why it's important."

They used simple analogies and interactive activities to explain concepts like blockchain, mining, and smart contracts. The kids were engaged, asking questions and participating eagerly.

One of the highlights was a hands-on activity where the kids created their own simple smart contracts using a basic coding platform. They were thrilled to see how their code could automatically execute agreements, just like they had learned in the Cryptoverse.

As the club grew, they decided to take on a project to create a digital art gallery using NFTs. Each member created a unique piece of digital art, which they then turned into NFTs. The kids were amazed to see their artwork displayed in a virtual gallery, and some even traded their NFTs with each other.

Max and Lily's Crypto Kids Club became a hit in their town, inspiring other kids to explore technology and cryptocurrency. They held regular meetings, workshops, and even invited guest speakers who were experts in the field.

Their journey through the Cryptoverse had not only taught them valuable lessons but had also ignited a passion for sharing their knowledge and helping others. They realized that the true power of cryptocurrency was not just in the technology itself, but in its potential to bring people together, inspire creativity, and empower individuals.

One afternoon, as they were preparing for another club meeting, Max looked at Lily and smiled. "We've come a long way from that dusty old computer in the attic."

Lily nodded, her eyes shining with satisfaction. "And this is just the beginning. Who knows what other adventures await us in the Cryptoverse?"

Max held up the special token Crypton had given them. "Whatever comes next, we're ready."

Just then, Max's computer screen flickered to life, displaying a series of strange symbols and a message: "Warning: Anomalous Activity Detected in the Cryptoverse."

Lily's eyes widened. "Do you think it's Hackzor?"

Max frowned. "I don't know, but we should find out. Let's finish this meeting and then check it out."

Their journey through the Cryptoverse had ended, but it seemed that a new adventure was already beginning. With the knowledge and skills they had gained, Max and Lily were determined to continue exploring, learning, and sharing their passion for technology and cryptocurrency with others. As they welcomed the new members of the Crypto Kids Club, they knew they were on the right path to making a difference in their community and beyond.

As they finished setting up for the meeting, they couldn't help but feel a thrill of anticipation for the challenges and discoveries that lay ahead. The Cryptoverse was calling them back, and they were ready to answer.

EPILOGUE

To help others understand and explore the world of cryptocurrency, Max and Lily created a glossary of terms and some fun activities.

Glossary of Cryptocurrency Terms

Blockchain: A digital ledger that records all transactions made with a particular cryptocurrency. It's like a public record that anyone can see, but it's secured using complex mathematical algorithms.

Cryptocurrency: A type of digital or virtual money that uses cryptography for security. Unlike traditional money issued by governments, cryptocurrencies are decentralized and operate on the blockchain.

Decentralized Finance (DeFi): A system of financial services that operates on the blockchain, allowing people to lend, borrow, and earn interest without the need for traditional banks.

NFT (Non-Fungible Token): A unique digital item stored on the blockchain. Unlike regular cryptocurrencies, which are identical and can be exchanged on a one-to-one basis, NFTs are one-of-a-kind and cannot be replaced with something else.

Smart Contract: A self-executing contract with the terms of the agreement directly written into code. Smart contracts run on the blockchain and automatically execute when the conditions are met.

Staking: The process of lending your cryptocurrency to a DeFi platform to earn interest. It's like putting your money in a savings account and earning interest.

Liquidity Pool: A collection of cryptocurrency tokens locked in a smart contract that provides liquidity, or ease of trading, for decentralized exchanges.

Collateral: Something valuable you offer as a guarantee when borrowing cryptocurrency. If you fail to repay the loan, the lender can take your collateral.

Interest Rate: The extra money you earn when you lend your cryptocurrency or the cost you pay when you borrow it. Interest rates in DeFi are determined by supply and demand.

Volatility: The degree to which the price of a cryptocurrency can fluctuate. High volatility means the price can change rapidly and unpredictably.

FINAL NOTE FROM MAX AND LILY

"We hope you enjoyed our adventure through the Cryptoverse as much as we did! Remember, the world of cryptocurrency is full of exciting possibilities, and there's always more to learn. Keep exploring, stay curious, and never stop asking questions. Who knows what incredible discoveries await you next?"

Made in the USA
Middletown, DE
30 November 2024

65752376R00042